1

Safety Skills

Whether you are home alone, watching younger brothers or sisters, or babysitting, it is important that you know how to stay safe.

2

Child Care Skills

When you babysit, you are the substitute parent. Different ages require you to do different tasks.

First Aid & Rescue Skills

Injuries are the leading cause of death in children up to age 5, but children of **every** age need protection.

3

4

Life & Business Skills

Success on the job depends on three things: being prepared, being responsible, and being considerate.

CONTENTS

SAFETY SKILLS

Whether you are home alone, watching younger brothers or sisters, or babysitting, it is important that you know how to stay safe.

Rule #1

When you are home alone, watching younger brothers and sisters, or babysitting, always practice safe habits for:

- Indoor Safety
- Outdoor Safety
- Online Safety
- Personal Safety

Safe habits save lives!

Rule #2

When you leave home, always make sure your parent or guardian knows:

- Who you will be with
- What you will be doing
- Where you will be
- When you will return home
- How you are getting to where you're going (and back home)

Rule #3

Call your parent or a back-up adult to come get you if you are in an unsafe situation.

- Use the safety signal: "I'm ready to be picked up now."

The safety signal is a secret code for "Please pick me up immediately. I'll explain later." Share this safety signal with your parent now so that you can use this safety signal to alert your parent when you need to be picked up immediately because you feel unsafe, no questions asked.

DO YOU HAVE A SAFE WAY TO GET WHERE YOU'RE GOING?

- Walking short distances in daylight, or with a companion at night in well-lit areas
- Riding in a car with a parent or other safe adult
- Taking public transportation – if you are experienced and your parent approves

SAFESITTER

SAFETY SKILLS

Indoor Safety

A lot can go wrong inside the house! When you are home alone or babysitting, follow these guidelines:

- Never use matches or lighters for any reason.
- Avoid using the stove to cook. Instead, make snacks and meals that do not require cooking, or use a microwave if necessary.
- Lock all doors and windows and close the curtains or blinds after dark. Do not answer the door unless you are expecting a visitor.
- Leave family pets alone, especially when they're eating, sleeping, or if they're caring for their puppies or kittens. Let unfamiliar pets see you and sniff you before you pet them.
- Make sure you know where a flashlight is in cases of weather related emergencies or power failures.
- Supervise young children in the bathroom, keep the toilet lid down, and don't give baths while you are babysitting. Remember that children can drown in just a few inches of water.

Outdoor Safety

It can be particularly challenging to stay safe outdoors, where traffic, playground equipment, and animals can create unsafe situations. Stay safe by following these guidelines:

- Go inside and lock the doors if a stranger approaches you or you see anyone or anything suspicious while playing outside. Take the children with you if you are babysitting.
- Call 9-1-1 if you see anyone or anything suspicious in the area.
- Watch younger children at all times on playground equipment.
- Stay out of the street when playing, especially in high traffic areas.
- Don't approach unfamiliar animals.
- Remain motionless when approached by an unfamiliar dog. Don't make eye contact, run, or scream.
- Never babysit at a home with a pool or swimming area unless you can swim. Don't allow children to swim or use a wading pool while you are babysitting. Keep small children away from pools, ponds, or other bodies of water.

Online Safety

Your safety could be at risk any time you go online. To protect your privacy and keep yourself safe, follow these guidelines:

- Use strong passwords and change them regularly.
- Make sure you understand and utilize privacy settings.
- Avoid suspicious emails, attachments, websites, and online advertisements.
- Don't give out personal information to people you don't know personally.
- Follow the rules and policies established by each program, game, or app you use.
- Treat people with respect, just as you would if you were talking to them in person.
- Report cyber-bullying, abusive behavior, and inappropriate content.
- Share your online activities with your parent.

Personal Safety

Whether you are alone or with others, take steps to protect your personal safety by following these guidelines:

- Have a cell phone with you or have access to a landline if you are home alone, watching younger brothers and sisters, or babysitting.
- Avoid being with anyone who you suspect has abused alcohol or drugs. Slurred speech, unsteady walking, or loud, rowdy behavior may be signs that someone is under the influence.
- Stay away from any person who makes you feel uncomfortable by the way they are talking to you or touching you. Tell the person they are making you feel uncomfortable, leave the room, and tell your parent or other safe adult.
- Be aware if there are guns in the home. Treat every gun like it is loaded and ready to fire. Don't touch a gun that you find in the home.
- Call your parent if you see or suspect illegal drugs in a home.
- Do not answer phone calls from people or phone numbers you do not know. Let the call go to voicemail.

IF YOU ARE BABYSITTING, ALWAYS CALL THE EMPLOYER AS SOON AS POSSIBLE AFTER YOU HAVE RESPONDED TO AN UNSAFE SITUATION.

Even when you are careful, things can happen. Here is some guidance on what to do in unsafe situations:

Break-in

- Call 9-1-1 if the home security alarm goes off or as soon as possible after a break-in.
- If someone breaks into the house, cooperate with the thief. Don't try to fight back or get a weapon, even if you know where one is stored.

Fire

- If you see or suspect fire in the house: stay calm, stay low, and immediately go outside, taking any children with you. Once outside, call 9-1-1 from a cell phone or neighbor's house, and stay outside until help arrives. Don't re-enter the building.

Power Outage

- If the power goes out, stay calm and find a flashlight.
- Call a back-up adult for help.

Smell of Gas or Smoke

- Go outside immediately, taking all children with you, then call 9-1-1 and stay outside until help arrives. Don't re-enter the building.
- Never ignore a smoke or carbon monoxide alarm. Call 9-1-1 and stay outside until help arrives.

Weather Emergencies

- If there is an earthquake, stay calm. If outside, stay in an open area away from buildings, trees, and power lines. If you are inside, take cover under a sturdy desk or table. Hold onto it and be prepared to move with it. Be prepared for additional earthquakes, called aftershocks. Stay in your area until the shaking stops.
- If there is a tornado, stay calm and move to the basement if possible, or to an interior room without windows, such as a bathroom. Take a battery operated radio, smartphone, or other electronic device with you to access weather or safety instructions.

Go to **safesitter.org** for important reminders about handling these and other unsafe situations.

Review

What are the three rules that will help you stay safe?

What is the safety signal you should use if you are in an unsafe situation?

Why should you be careful of what you post online?

CHILD CARE SKILLS

When you babysit, you are the substitute parent. Different ages require you to do different tasks. You may have to do some child care tasks that you do not enjoy—like changing dirty diapers. Before you accept a babysitting job, think about how the age of the child will affect your duties.

Warning!

THE CARE AND HANDLING OF INFANTS LESS THAN 6 MONTHS OLD IS VERY DEMANDING.

You should not accept the responsibility for care of an infant younger than 6 months until you have had at least 2 years' experience babysitting for older infants and children.

Age Groups

Early childhood is divided into 4 major age groups:

- Infants, under 1 year
- Toddlers, 1 to 2 years old
- Preschoolers, 3 to 5 years old
- School age, 6 to 10 years old

Before you accept a babysitting job, ask yourself if you are ready, willing, and able to handle all the care the child requires. Use the Safe Sitter® Guide to Child Development and the Safe Sitter® Guide to Child Care Duties to help you decide if you should accept a job.

Know the ages and stages!

Safe Sitter® Guide to Child Development

	INFANTS under 1 year old	**TODDLERS** 1 to 2 years old	**PRESCHOOLERS** 3 to 5 years old	**SCHOOL AGE** 6 to 10 years old
Movement	Cannot walk Must be carried	Beginning to walk Fall easily Can't do stairs alone	Can walk and run Use riding toys	Ride bikes—must wear a helmet Play sports
Speech	Cannot talk Make cooing sounds like "ahh" and "ooh"	Use single words and simple sentences like "Me do it" May be hard to understand	Ask questions Enjoy talking Still learning to speak clearly	Talk well Read
Safety	Cannot recognize danger **Require constant watching** Depend completely on you	Cannot recognize danger **Require constant watching**	May recognize danger but **require constant watching**	Know how to stay safe but may take risks
Following the Rules	Too young to know or follow rules Require patience on your part	Too young to know or follow rules Require patience on your part	Usually follow rules	Almost always follow rules
Behavior Challenges	Cries to communicate	May cry when employer leaves May have temper tantrums May repeat "No"	May hit or kick when frustrated May ignore rules	May argue or fight with siblings May challenge rules
Ideas for Comfort	Cuddle Gently rock Give pacifier Talk softly Slowly walk with infant	Hold or cuddle Give special blanket or stuffed animal Pat child's back Sing songs	Give special blanket or stuffed animal Tell short, happy stories using child's name Suggest a favorite game or activity Sing songs	Give favorite toy Distract with funny stories, books, or board games Sing songs

CHILD CARE SKILLS

Safe Sitter® Guide to Child Care Duties

	INFANTS under 1 year old **Depend completely on you**	**TODDLERS** 1 to 2 years old **Mostly depend on you**	**PRESCHOOLERS** 3 to 5 years old **Mostly able to do things alone**	**SCHOOL AGE** 6 to 10 years old **Able to do things alone**
Bedtime	Sleep on back in crib with no pillows, blankets, or toys Need diaper changed at nap/nighttime	Resist bedtime Need routine	Usually cooperate Need sitter to be firm and consistent Need 5-minute warning	Know the rules Need 30-minute warning
Entertainment	Like soft noises Like being walked and talked to	Have short attention span Enjoy simple games, balls, and puzzles	Love pretending, stories, and easy board games	Like active play, coloring, and crafts
Snacks/Meals	Take bottles Need to be fed baby food	Need hands washed by sitter Are messy eaters Need to be strapped in high chair	Need reminders to wash hands Are able to use spoon and cup when eating	May push snacking rules
Toileting	Wear diapers Need frequent changes	Resist diaper changes May be in process of potty training	Can probably go to bathroom alone but may need help Need reminders to use bathroom and wash hands	Younger school-age children need reminders to use bathroom, especially at bedtime Need reminders to wash hands

MATCHING ACTIVITY: What age?

Draw a line from the behavior to the age group most likely to use that behavior.

What age is likely to . . .

Need everything to be done by you?   School age

Be resistant?   Toddler

Be cooperative but need frequent reminders?   Infant

Know the rules, but push them?   Preschooler

SNACK OR MEAL IDEAS

- Cheese and crackers
- Applesauce
- Pretzels
- Yogurt
- Cottage cheese with pineapple slices
- Whole grain cereal with berries and milk

Check out **safesitter.org** for more ideas!

Children's Routines

The **BEST** babysitters know the child's routines. Before the employer leaves the house, ask about BEST—**B**edtime, **E**ntertainment, **S**nacks/Meals, **T**oileting.

Bedtime

Follow employer's rules.

If caring for an infant, be sure to place the infant on his or her back when putting the infant to bed, even for short naps. Let the child unwind as bedtime nears. Ask about and follow the child's bedtime routine. Ask what to do if the child has sleeping problems like sleepwalking.

Entertainment

Children love active play. Ask employer for entertainment ideas.

Never let a toddler out of your sight. Never let a child play with latex balloons or any toy smaller than the child's fist, as these are choking hazards.

Don't allow children to play on stairs, balconies, or landings. Only use stair gates as directed by employer. Don't let children of any age take any risks like climbing trees or jumping from high places. Get employers' permission for activities like skateboarding, using scooters, or playing on a trampoline. Ask employer about rules for using electronic devices.

Snacks/Meals

Be sure you and the child wash hands before eating or preparing food.

Danger! Don't play games at mealtime because the child may giggle and choke on a mouthful of food. No smooth, round food that can slide down into the airway like hot dogs or grapes up to age 5. No hard food like hard candy up to age 5.

Because of food allergies, only give food provided by employer. Do not use the stove to prepare food. If using a microwave, let the food cool in the microwave a few minutes before you take it out. Test the temperature of all food to be sure it's not too hot.

Ask employer for meals and snacks that do not require cooking.

Toileting

Wear disposable gloves when changing diapers if they are available. Always change the child's diaper before putting the child to bed and when getting the child up. Dispose of diapers exactly as employer tells you.

Wash your hands after removing and disposing of gloves and after helping the child with toileting. Ask employer the words the child uses to signal they need to use the bathroom.

10 Steps to Changing Diapers

Changing a diaper is easier than you think. Ask the employer to show you how. Be sure to make eye contact and talk or sing with an infant. You may need safe toys to distract a toddler during the diaper change.

Safety comes first! Keep one hand on the infant at all times! Never leave the infant!

1. Choose a safe place to change the infant's diaper—on the floor on a changing pad or towel.

2. Make sure you have all the supplies you need—clean diaper, wipes, etc.—within reach first.

3. To remove the dirty diaper, undo the tabs first and gently slide the diaper from under the infant's bottom.

4. Gently wipe the infant from front to back with a washcloth or wipe. Be sure to get the little folds and creases clean.

5. Pat the infant dry with a clean washcloth or wipe to prevent diaper rash.

6. Gently lift the infant's legs with one hand and slide a clean diaper under infant's bottom with the other hand. Be sure you have the side with the adhesive tabs underneath the infant.

7. Before you fasten the tabs, make sure the front of the diaper is centered between the legs and pulled up to the same level as in the back— usually around the level of the belly button in the front.

8. To prevent leaks, bring the adhesive strips forward and fasten them snugly on the front of the diaper so there are no gaps. Be careful not to stick the adhesive tape to the infant's skin.

9. Roll up the old diaper—and wipes—onto itself in a ball. Fasten the tabs to secure it. Dispose of the old diaper and wipes as directed by the employer. One option is to put the old diaper in a plastic bag and tie it closed. Then put it in the trash.

10. Always wash your hands with soap and water after you have disposed of the diaper.

WASHING HANDS

Wet hands. Apply soap and rub together vigorously for 15-20 seconds (the time it takes to sing "Happy Birthday" twice). Rinse well under running water. Dry with paper towel. If soap and water are not available, use hand sanitizer and rub hands together until completely dry. Do not let the child suck on or play with hand sanitizer bottle.

Entertainment Ideas

INFANTS
under 1 year old

Infants have short attention spans and are frequently interested in a toy or activity for only a few minutes at a time. Be patient with infants. Do not expect more than they are capable of.

6 Months to 1 Year
- Play games where infant drops object and you pick it up. Make sure object is not breakable.
- Play nursery games like Peek-a-Boo and Patty-Cake.
- Play Hide-and-Seek with objects.
- Walk around the house looking at and naming things.
- Roll a ball to infant.
- Take stroller ride if weather is nice.

NEED MORE IDEAS?
Check out **safesitter.org** for games and activities you can do with kids of all ages when you're babysitting!

TODDLERS
1 to 2 years old

Toddlers can be lots of fun or lots of work. They are constantly on the move—exploring, investigating, and copying grown-ups. Their attempts to do more than they can do often lead to frustration with crying, temper tantrums, and even biting. Their attention spans are short and they enjoy frequent activity changes.

Active Play
- Build with blocks and knock them down.
- Play with action toys they push or pull.
- Play with toys that let them play grown-up like telephones, tool sets, and dish sets.
- Play outdoors with balls or just go exploring.
- Make music with toy instruments.
- Play simple games like Hide-and-Seek. Hide so child can see part of you. Beware of safety hazards like electrical outlets, stairs, and streets.
- Walk around the house looking for everything that is a particular color or shape.

Quiet Play
- Play with soft stuffed animals.
- Sing children's songs and finger games like Itsy-Bitsy Spider.

PRESCHOOLERS
3 to 5 years old

Preschoolers are finally able to get where they want to go and do what they want to do on their own. They have strong likes and dislikes. Be sure to ask about favorite toys and play activities. Pretend play can keep a preschooler happy for 30 minutes to an hour. Active games are an ideal change of pace when child becomes bored.

Active Play
- Read a book and choose parts to act out.
- Put on a play or talent show using stuffed animals for the audience.
- Play with Lego® blocks or other construction toys.
- Go on a scavenger hunt.
- Play tag or Hide-and-Seek.
- Play with riding toys. Be careful to supervise.

Quiet Play
- Play easy board games.
- Play imaginative games like school, store, or spaceships.
- Play I Spy or other guessing games.
- Listen to stories that you make up or read. No scary stories. Young children may be extremely frightened and have nightmares or trouble going to sleep.

SCHOOL AGE
6 to 10 years old

Doing things with school-age children can be a lot of fun for both of you. You may have forgotten how much fun some of these activities are.

Inside Activities
- Play board games.
- Play pencil-and-paper games like Tic-Tac-Toe.
- Make up stories with words that rhyme.
- Make up games like, "Name everything you can think of that begins with C."
- Play with crafts or activity books.
- Read.
- Play with Lego® blocks or other construction toys.

Outside Activities
- Jump rope.
- Play games like Mother May I, Red Light/Green Light, Simon Says, and Hokey-Pokey.
- Play catch, basketball, soccer, or Frisbee®.

Behavior Management

Stay in control of yourself.

Sometimes, the behavior of children you are caring for can be challenging or frustrating. Managing this behavior is the hardest part of taking care of children. While it may be frustrating, you must be able to control your own behavior. This means you must be patient and control your temper when you're taking care of young children. Always use a pleasant yet firm tone of voice when dealing with challenging behavior. Never use physical punishment.

Stay in control of the children.

Children who are out of control may harm themselves or others. Young children are still learning to control their words, actions, and feelings. As a babysitter, you accept responsibility to be in control of the behavior of the children you are watching.

Babysitting for brothers and sisters can be especially difficult. You can make it easier for everyone if you approach the job determined to make the time fun, do special things that they enjoy, and be fair with the rules. Your parent can help you by making it clear that you are in charge.

4 Rules You Must Follow

1. You must be in control of yourself. Call your parent or back-up adult for relief if you are losing control.
2. You must be in control of the children. Call for help if you can't control the children.
3. You must never use physical punishment like shaking, slapping, spanking, pinching, poking, or hitting. Shaking a young child can cause permanent brain damage. NEVER SHAKE AN INFANT.
4. You must never hurt with words. Be firm but not harsh.

PREVENT CHALLENGING BEHAVIOR BEFORE IT HAPPENS!

- Praise good behavior.
- Be consistent with rules.
- Know the ages and stages and keep expectations reasonable.
- Act quickly to help a child who is losing control.
- Be creative in getting the child to cooperate.
- Get help quickly if you are unable to control the child's behavior.

Behavior Management Tips

1. **Provide Comfort**
   Make sure the child isn't tired, hungry, or needing a diaper change. Offer the child a favorite stuffed animal or doll, give the child a hug, or speak to them with soothing words.
   EXAMPLE: Sophia, 3, wakes up from a nightmare and screams for her parent. The Safe Sitter® speaks to Sophia in a soothing voice, offers Sophia her favorite doll, and tells Sophia a story to help Sophia fall asleep again.

2. **Distract**
   Use a toy, story, or song to distract the child's attention.
   EXAMPLE: Sara, 2, cries when her mother leaves. The Safe Sitter® picks up Sara's stuffed bear and sings while she makes the bear dance. Sara is entertained; she doesn't notice that her mother left.

3. **Give Choices**
   Offer the child acceptable choices while still insisting on what needs to be done.
   EXAMPLE: Denzel, 4, takes a ball from his brother. The Safe Sitter® says, "You need to give the ball back to your brother. Do you want me to hand it to him or would you like to?"

4. **Make a Game**
   Turn something that needs to be done into a game.
   EXAMPLE: Jacob, 3, doesn't want to pick up his toys. The Safe Sitter® says, "You pick up the toys on one side of the room, and I'll pick up the toys on the other side and we'll see who gets done first."

5. **When…Then**
   Promise something the child wants to do after the child does something they do not want to do.
   EXAMPLE: Ella, 6, doesn't want to get ready for bed. The Safe Sitter® says, "When you put on your pajamas, then we'll read your favorite book."

6. **Take a Break/Start Over**
   Take a Break/Start Over is a way to help stop problem behavior and help a child get back in control. Taking a break allows time for the child to think about their behavior. Break time should be short—one minute for each year of the child's age. Break time can be time sitting in a chair, time without a toy, or time without television. It helps to separate the child from other children. Never put the child in the dark. Also, this tip should not be used for a child under the age of 2. When break time has ended, help the child return to play by saying, "Okay, let's start over."
   EXAMPLE: Carlos, 3, is playing rough with a toy car. The Safe Sitter® warns him to stop but he doesn't. The Safe Sitter® says, "Stop or I'll put the car away." He still doesn't stop. The Safe Sitter® tells Carlos he needs to take a break from playing with the car and puts the car out of his reach for three minutes. After three minutes, the Safe Sitter® gives Carlos his car and says, "Okay, let's start over."

Behavior Management

STAY IN CONTROL OF YOURSELF. STAY IN CONTROL OF THE CHILDREN.

CALL 9-1-1 FOR THREAT TO LIFE
- Breath holding if child loses consciousness or appears to have seizure
- Child needing rescue from tree, roof, window ledge, etc.
- Child threatening to hurt self or others with a weapon
- Child threatening to start a fire
- Physical fighting where serious harm is a risk, especially with older children

MAKING THE PHONE CALL TO 9-1-1

Give the alert: **"I am babysitting. This is an emergency!"**

Answer all the questions that 9-1-1 asks.

Be prepared to say:

1. Address where you are located with name of town and special instructions to find house or apartment
2. Your name
3. Phone number you are calling from with area code
4. The problem
5. What you have done

Tell 9-1-1 if you're calling from a cell phone.

Call employer after 9-1-1 arrives.

MAKE YOUR DECISION!

MAKE YOUR CALL!

MAKING THE PHONE CALL TO BACK-UP ADULT

Give the alert: **"I am babysitting. I need help now!"**

Tell the back-up adult:

1. The problem
2. What you have done
3. Ask back-up adult to come help

Call employer to tell employer about any problem that required assistance from back-up adult.

When employer comes home ask for suggestions on how to handle the problem in the future.

MAKE YOUR DECISION!

MAKE YOUR CALL!

Behavior Management

STAY IN CONTROL OF YOURSELF. STAY IN CONTROL OF THE CHILDREN.

Behavior Management

STAY IN CONTROL OF YOURSELF. STAY IN CONTROL OF THE CHILDREN.

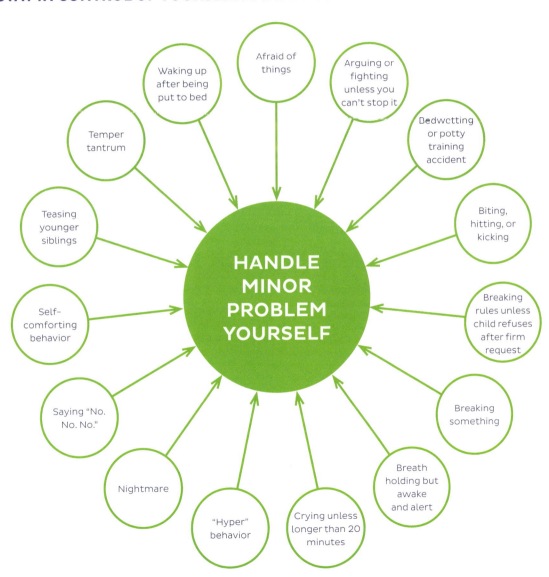

Handle minor problem yourself:
- Waking up after being put to bed
- Afraid of things
- Arguing or fighting unless you can't stop it
- Bedwetting or potty training accident
- Biting, hitting, or kicking
- Breaking rules unless child refuses after firm request
- Breaking something
- Breath holding but awake and alert
- Crying unless longer than 20 minutes
- "Hyper" behavior
- Nightmare
- Saying "No. No. No."
- Self-comforting behavior
- Teasing younger siblings
- Temper tantrum

REFER TO THE SAFE SITTER® BEHAVIOR AID CHART AND FOLLOW DIRECTIONS EXACTLY

When employer comes home, tell employer about any behavior issues, even if you have handled the situation and it is completely taken care of.

Tell employer:
1. The problem
2. What you did
3. How the child reacted

MAKE YOUR DECISION!

MAKE YOUR CALL!

Behavior Aid Chart

INFANTS (under 1 year old)

Crying:
Handle yourself. Check to be sure infant is not hungry, wet, sleepy, or in pain. Comfort infant by cuddling, gently rocking, softly talking, slowly walking infant, or offering pacifier. **Call back-up adult** if infant cries for more than 20 minutes. Never shake or punish an infant for crying.

TODDLERS (1 to 2 years old)

Biting or Hitting:
Handle yourself. Kneel down to child's eye level and be sure you have child's attention. Tell child "No biting. Biting hurts." or "No hitting. Hitting hurts." Never bite or hit a child to show how it feels. If skin is broken, see Safe Sitter® First Aid Chart.

Breath Holding:
Prevent by distraction if possible. **Handle yourself** if child is awake and alert. Watch for return of regular breathing and activity. **Call 9-1-1** if child loses consciousness or appears to have a convulsion or seizure.

Crying at Bedtime:
Handle yourself. Follow employer's routine exactly. Use comforting techniques such as a night light, stuffed animal, bedtime story, or special blanket.

Crying When Employer Leaves:
Handle yourself. Do your part to prevent by arriving in time to play with child while employer is still home. Distract child with toy or game. Comfort child by holding child and cuddling child if child will allow or offering favorite blanket or toy.

"Hyper" Behavior:
Handle yourself. Help child use the energy through an active game, or change activities if child is bored or frustrated.

Potty Training Accident:
Handle yourself. Clean child and change child's clothes if needed. Do not scold or tease child.

Saying "No. No. No.":
Handle yourself. Respect the "no" if child really means it. Do not make fun of child who says no to everything.

Temper Tantrum:
Handle yourself. Ignore child until the tantrum has ended. If child falls to the ground kicking, move things out of the way so child will not be harmed and things won't get broken. When tantrum ends, distract child with game or play.

Thumb or Finger Sucking, Pacifier, Taking Bedtime Bottle:
Handle yourself. Don't worry about this self-comforting behavior. Do not scold or tease child.

Waking Up After Being Put to Bed:
Handle yourself. Prevent by following child's bedtime routine. Go to child's room and talk to child. Tell child it's time for sleeping, not playing. If child cries for employer, remind child that employer will be coming home. Comfort child by patting child's back, singing, or telling a short, happy story.

PRESCHOOLERS (3 to 5 years old)

Afraid of Things:
Handle yourself. Comfort child with distractions such as story or game.

Bedwetting:
Handle yourself. Do your part to prevent embarrassment for child by reminding child to go to bathroom before bed. Help child change to clean clothes and change the sheets or place dry towels over the wet spot in the bed. Do not scold or tease child.

Breaking Rules or Not Listening:
Handle yourself. Remind child that you are following employer's rules. Be firm. Try giving child choices or making a game of what you want child to do. Remind child of the consequences for breaking rules. Use Take a Break/Start Over if necessary. **Call back-up adult** if that doesn't work.

Breaking Something:
Handle yourself. Pick up pieces and put them where no one will be hurt. If you are unable to keep child safely away from the danger while you clean up, then block off the area.

Hitting or Kicking:
Handle yourself. Separate child from others. Allow child to Take a Break/Start Over. Remind child to use words instead of hitting or kicking when angry.

Locking You Out of House or Room:
Call back-up adult.

Nightmare:
Handle yourself. Comfort child. If possible, calm child without turning on the light. It may help to have the child go to the bathroom, take a few sips of water, or distract child with a pleasant bedtime story.

Potty Training Accident:
Handle yourself. Clean child and change child's clothes if needed. Do not scold or tease child.

SCHOOL AGE (6 to 10 years old)

Arguing or Fighting:
Handle yourself. Settle the argument as fairly as possible. If physical fighting, separate the children. **Call back-up adult** if you are unable to stop the fight. **Call 9-1-1** if serious harm is a risk.

Breaking Rules or Not Listening:
Do your part to prevent by asking employer to go over rules in front of child. Before leaving, employer needs to stress that you are in charge and children must cooperate. **Handle yourself.** Be firm, and remind child that you have the responsibility to enforce employer's rules. Warn child of the consequences for breaking rules. **Call back-up adult** if child still refuses to follow the rules.

Child Needing Rescue from Tree, Roof, Window Ledge, etc.:
Call 9-1-1.

Inviting Friends in Without Permission:
Handle yourself. Remind child in private of the house rules. Allow child to tell friends they have to leave. **Call back-up adult** if child refuses.

Leaving Home Without Permission:
Call back-up adult immediately and report child's behavior.

Threatening to Hurt Self or Others:
Call 9-1-1 if child has weapon which could cause harm or if child is in physical danger.

Threatening to Start a Fire:
Call 9-1-1.

Teasing Younger Siblings:
Handle yourself. Distract older sibling with a request that acknowledges the age and abilities of older child.

EXAMPLE: "Could you check to make sure the doors are locked?" Suggest an activity you can do together after younger child goes to bed. If distraction doesn't work, talk with older child privately, stating firmly and seriously, that the teasing must stop or you will report it to employer.

Review

What are the four age groups?

What age groups need constant watching?

What are the routines that the BEST babysitter knows about?

What are the 4 rules that you must follow?

What are the 6 Behavior Management Tips?

FIRST AID & RESCUE SKILLS

Injuries are the leading cause of death in children up to age 5, but children of **every** age need protection. As a babysitter, you accept the responsibility to provide that protection. You must think of yourself as a bodyguard.

You need to be with young children every minute they're awake. Young children—even infants—can easily place themselves at risk for injury or even death.

Prevent injuries before they happen!

- Look for danger in the area where the child is playing.
- Remove the danger when possible, or block the child's path to danger.
- Use child safety aids such as high chair safety belts and safety gates.
- Watch children who are preschoolers or younger at all times when they are awake and check on them at least once per hour when they are asleep.
- Act quickly to rescue a child who is moving into danger.
- Be especially aware in kitchens and bathrooms, where most injuries occur.

Be aware of safety hazards that can be dangerous for children of all ages:
- Latex balloons
- Electrical outlets
- Stairs
- Hard candy
- Medicine
- Cleaning products

Guide to Common Dangers

Infants
- rolling off changing table
- choking
- poisoning

Toddlers
- falling and hitting furniture
- falling down stairs
- drowning
- choking
- poisoning

Preschoolers
- getting too close to dangerous machinery (lawnmowers, shredders, etc.)
- falling off play equipment
- choking
- poisoning

School Age
- falling off a bike
- getting hurt while playing sports or outside games
- choking

FIRST AID & RESCUE SKILLS

ALLERGIES

Some children have allergies – their bodies react to certain substances (like pollen, pet dander, or even foods such as nuts) as if that substance is harmful. The allergic reaction can differ from person to person, depending on the severity of the allergy.

If you are babysitting a child who has an allergy that could be life threatening, ask the employer if the child has an auto-injector such as an EpiPen®, where it is located, and if the child knows how to use it.

MATCHING ACTIVITY: What age?

Draw a line from the danger to the age group most likely to be at risk.

What age is likely to . . .

Roll off of a changing table or sofa — School age

Ride their bike into the street without looking — Infant

Fall down stairs that are not protected by a safety gate — Preschool

Chew on medication thinking it is candy — Toddler

Be aware of a child's exposure to possible allergens:

- Bees
- Nuts
- Wheat products
- Dairy products
- Animal dander

Injury Management
STAY CALM. STAY SAFE. PROVIDE COMFORT.

CALL 9-1-1 FOR THREAT TO LIFE
- Broken bone with deformity and break in skin or cold/blue skin below injured part
- Burn with blisters over large area or any electrical burn
- Cut that is pumping blood rapidly
- Loss of consciousness—becomes unaware of surroundings, not able to respond
- No breathing—sudden infant death syndrome
- Poisoning with symptoms
- Puncture wound due to large object
- Serious head, neck, or back injury
- Trouble breathing from choking, drowning, electrical shock, asthma, severe allergic reaction, convulsion or seizure

MAKING THE PHONE CALL TO 9-1-1

Give the alert: **"I am babysitting. This is an emergency!"**

Answer all the questions that 9-1-1 asks.

Be prepared to say:
1. Address where you are located with name of town and special instructions to find house or apartment
2. Your name
3. Phone number you are calling from with area code
4. The problem
5. What you have done

Tell 9-1-1 if you're calling from a cell phone.

Call employer after 9-1-1 arrives.

MAKE YOUR DECISION!

MAKE YOUR CALL!

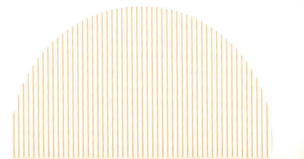

MAKING THE PHONE CALL TO BACK-UP ADULT

Give the alert: **"I am babysitting. I need help now!"**

Tell the back-up adult:

1. The problem
2. What you have done
3. Ask back-up adult to come help

If you suspect poisoning but there are no symptoms, call Poison Center 800-222-1222 while the back-up adult is on the way. Have your Safe Sitter® First Aid Chart available to show the back-up adult.

Call employer to tell employer about any problem that required assistance from back-up adult.

MAKE YOUR DECISION!

MAKE YOUR CALL!

Injury Management

STAY CALM. STAY SAFE. PROVIDE COMFORT.

Ask back-up adult to come help for:
- Vomiting—not spitting up
- Animal or human bite
- Asthma if child is wheezing with NO trouble breathing
- Bruise over large area or scrape with gravel or dirt in it
- Possible sprain, fracture, or broken bone with no break in skin
- Cut that is on face or is large or with edges spread widely apart
- Poisoning without symptoms (Also call Poison Center 800-222-1222)
- Eye or ear injury
- Nosebleed that is heavy or lasts more than 5 minutes
- Fever
- Minor puncture wound
- Knocked out or broken permanent tooth
- Minor burn or scald
- Minor allergic reaction—hives if limited to a small area

Injury Management

STAY CALM. STAY SAFE. PROVIDE COMFORT.

REFER TO THE SAFE SITTER® FIRST AID CHART AND FOLLOW DIRECTIONS EXACTLY

When employer comes home, tell employer about any injury or problem, even if you have handled the situation and it is completely taken care of.

Tell employer:

1. The problem
2. What you did
3. How the child reacted

MAKE YOUR DECISION!

MAKE YOUR CALL!

Safe Sitter® First Aid Chart

STAY CALM. STAY SAFE. PROVIDE COMFORT.

Allergic Reaction

Call 9-1-1 for severe allergic reaction—trouble breathing or swallowing, loss of consciousness, weakness, nausea, vomiting, fainting, hives—red, itchy bumps on skin—over entire body, or severe swelling of eyes, lips, or tongue. **Call back-up adult** for hives limited to a small area.

Asthma

Call 9-1-1 if child's lips are pale or blue or child has difficulty breathing or talking. **Call back-up adult** if child is wheezing with NO trouble breathing. Adult can help with medicines.

Bite or Sting

Animal Bite or Human Bite

Call back-up adult to evaluate seriousness. Adult should wash wound with soap and lots of water. If skin is broken, child will need further treatment.

Insect Sting

Call 9-1-1 if signs of severe allergic reaction. **Handle yourself** if swelling and redness are limited to site of the sting. If stinger is visible, immediately scrape—do not pull—with your fingernail to remove. Cover with clean cloth dipped in cold water.

Breath Holding

Handle yourself if child is awake and alert. Watch for return of regular breathing and activity. **Call 9-1-1** if child loses consciousness or appears to have a convulsion or seizure.

Broken Bone/Fracture/Sprain

Do not move child if you suspect a broken bone! Suspect a broken bone if child falls and has any of the following: won't stop crying, won't use injured part, obvious swelling or deformity. A broken bone should not be moved until it has been splinted.

Call 9-1-1 if there is obvious swelling or deformity with a break in skin or if area below injured part is cold or blue. **Call back-up adult** to help evaluate for possible broken bone.

Bruise

Call back-up adult for bruise over a large area, continued pain, or swelling. **Handle yourself** if bruise is small. Put plastic bag filled with ice on bruise with towel between ice and skin for at least 5 minutes. Decrease time if child resists and there is not much swelling.

Burn or Scald

Stop the burning process by removing child from contact with source of heat. Have child Stop, Drop and Roll if clothes are on fire. Pour cool water over clothes to stop further burning.

Call 9-1-1 if burn with blisters over large area. Do not apply any medicines. Do not break blisters. Do not use ice. Have child lie down, cover with clean sheet, and then blanket until 9-1-1 arrives. **Call back-up adult** if minor burn with or without blisters. Adult can place burned area in cool water or cover with clean cloth dipped in cold water until pain stops.

Electrical Burn or Shock

Do not touch child if child is still in contact with source of electricity. Pull plug from source of electricity if possible. If child is blue and not breathing and it is safe to touch the child, do CPR for 2 minutes and then **call 9-1-1**.

Convulsion or Seizure

Not responding to things or people and child's body stiffens, twitches, shakes, or child just stares. If child is blue and not breathing, do CPR for 2 minutes and then **call 9-1-1**. If child is breathing, roll child on side to prevent choking. Do not try to restrain movements. Protect child from injury by moving furniture or other objects away from child. Do not put or force any object into child's mouth.

Cut

If cut is pumping blood rapidly, place clean cloth over the entire wound and press firmly. Have child lie down. If blood comes through cloth, do not remove blood-soaked cloth. Cover with second cloth and continue to press firmly.

Call 9-1-1 as soon as active bleeding is under control or if you are unable to control bleeding quickly. Continue pressure until 9-1-1 arrives. **Call back-up adult** if cut is on the face or is large or the edges of cut are spread widely apart. Child may need medical care as soon as possible. Adult should use firm pressure with clean cloth over bleeding site to stop bleeding. **Handle yourself** if cut is small. Rinse with clean water. Pat dry and apply antibiotic ointment. Cover with BAND-AID® or bandage that will not stick to skin.

Drowning

Do not go into water that is deeper than your waist. Throw life jacket, piece of wood or anything that floats, as close as possible to child. If water is not deeper than your waist, pull child from water. If child is blue and not breathing, do CPR for 2 minutes and then **call 9-1-1**.

Eye and Ear Injury

Call back-up adult. Child will need medical care.

SAFESITTER PAGE 35

Fever

Call back-up adult if child's forehead feels hot to touch, child is sweating or shivering, child complains of feeling sick, or child looks sick. Do not take temperature. **Handle yourself** if child is hot from being in the sun or exercising in the heat. Get child to cooler, shaded area to rest. Give child water.

Head Injury

Do not move child who may have had serious head, neck, or back injury.

Call 9-1-1 if child has any loss of consciousness, convulsions, oozing blood or watery fluid from ears or nose, sleepiness, headache, vomiting, clumsiness, inability to move any body part, or change in speech or behavior. **Call back-up adult** if child has large cut, facial injuries, or won't stop crying. **Handle yourself** if bruise or small cut on scalp not involving face.

Loss of Consciousness

Becomes unaware of surroundings, not able to respond.

Call 9-1-1. Check for bleeding, head or neck injury, and breathing motions. If bleeding is controlled, no head or neck injury, and child is breathing, then roll child on side. Watch for trouble breathing. Keep child warm and do not give child anything to eat or drink.

Nosebleed

Handle yourself. Place child in sitting position leaning forward and squeeze outside of nostrils with thumb and first finger for 5 minutes. Have child sit quietly. **Call back-up adult** if bleeding continues after 5 minutes or bleeding is very heavy.

Poisoning

Any product or substance that can harm someone if used in the wrong way, by the wrong person, or in the wrong amount is a poison. Poison can enter the body through the eyes, ears, or skin or by breathing or swallowing something you shouldn't.

Call 9-1-1 if child takes anything that might be poison and immediately gags, vomits, becomes sleepy, has trouble breathing, has convulsions, or loss of consciousness. **Call back-up adult** and while adult is on the way **call Poison Center 800-222-1222** if child takes anything that might be poison but has no immediate symptoms. Have poison container available. Poison Center will tell you whether or not there is a problem and what to do.

Puncture Wound

Deep wound with small opening. Do not remove large object such as knife or stick.

Call 9-1-1 if puncture wound is due to large object. **Call back-up adult** for minor puncture wounds. Have adult wash with soap and water.

Scrape

Skinned area.

Handle yourself. Rinse with clean water for several minutes. Pat dry and apply antibiotic ointment. Cover with BAND-AID® or bandage that will not stick to skin. **Call back-up adult** if gravel or dirt is in skinned area and cannot be cleaned out.

Splinter

Long, thin, needle-like piece of glass, wood, or metal pushed through skin and into soft tissue beneath skin.

Handle yourself. Remove small splinter with tweezers if child will cooperate. After removing splinter, wash with soap and water. Do not soak splinter. Inform employer regardless of your success in removing splinter.

Tooth

Knocked Out or Broken Permanent Tooth

To stop bleeding, use clean, wet cloth and carefully apply pressure to area.

Call back-up adult immediately. Find tooth or tooth pieces. Have adult rinse tooth gently handling tooth by the top and not the root—part that would be in the gum. Place in cow's milk or clean water. Child will need dental attention immediately.

Baby Tooth

Handle yourself. If tooth falls out, have child rinse mouth with cold water. Save tooth for employer.

Vomiting

Have child lean forward, preferably over container such as wastebasket or bowl. Keep your mind on child—not on vomit or smell. When vomiting stops, help child to bathroom to wipe off vomit. Then take child with you to **call back-up adult.**

EMERGENCY SERVICES PHONE NUMBER: 9-1-1

POISON CENTER PHONE NUMBER: 800-222-1222

Employer needs to check for child's protection against tetanus—a very serious disease caused by infection of a wound resulting in muscle contractions which can prevent breathing—whenever skin is broken.

You need to protect yourself from contagious diseases by wearing disposable gloves whenever skin is broken or when you could come into contact with blood or other body fluids. Remember to wash your hands after removing and disposing of gloves. **Warning:** latex gloves should not be used with people who are allergic to latex rubber.

REMEMBER:

1. Call employer if you have called 9-1-1.
2. Call employer to tell employer about any problem that required assistance from back-up adult.
3. If in doubt, call employer.
4. When employer comes home, tell employer about any problem that you handled yourself.

Information on this First Aid Chart should not be used as a substitute for obtaining prompt help from 9-1-1 or from back-up adult.

FIRST AID & RESCUE SKILLS

Choking Child Rescue

1 YEAR OR OLDER

Coughing Helps!

Stay with the child, encourage coughing and be ready to rescue if the child:

- puts food or other object in mouth and begins to cough
- has sudden difficulty breathing—especially if the child is coughing

Choking Requires Help!

Act immediately if the child:

- is unable to breathe
- is unable to make a noise when trying to cough, cry, or talk and looks frightened
- has high-pitched, noisy breathing or is making gagging sound
- has bluish lips or skin is pale, blue, or grayish
- makes the choking sign—clutching neck

1. **Encourage the child to cough. Do not pat or slap the child on the back.** Ask an older child, "Are you choking?"
2. **Prepare to give abdominal thrusts** If the child nods "yes", is unable to cough or talk, or if cough becomes very weak. Tell the child you are going to help.
3. **Ask anyone who can to call 9-1-1 for help.** If you are alone, do not delay rescue attempts to make the call.
4. **Get in position to give abdominal thrusts.** Kneel or stand behind the child and put your arms around the child's body making sure your arms are under child's arms and below child's ribs.
5. **Give up to 5 abdominal thrusts.** Make a fist with one hand. Place thumb of your fist slightly above the child's belly button and well below the lower tip of breastbone. Grasp your fist with your other hand and "cough" for the child by giving up to 5 quick, forceful, upward abdominal thrusts. Say out loud, "Cough! Cough! Cough! Cough! Cough!"
6. **After every 5 abdominal thrusts:**
   - Check your hands to be sure they are in the correct position—slightly above the belly button and well below the lower tip of the breastbone.
   - Check your arms to be sure they are in the correct position under the child's arms and below the child's ribs.
   - Check the condition of the child.
7. **Don't give up.** Continue giving abdominal thrusts until the object is "coughed out" and the child can breathe, cough or talk, or until the child stops responding or loses consciousness.
8. **If the child loses consciousness, lower the child to the ground faceup and call 9-1-1** for further instructions.
9. If the child begins to breathe, cough, or talk, stop giving abdominal thrusts.
10. **Always call employer after 9-1-1 arrives** or if you have given abdominal thrusts.

Understanding Choking Child Rescue

How can I protect a child from choking?
The best protection is prevention. Remove objects that are choking hazards from the play area. Watch the child! Watch for danger!

Why is it important for me to stay calm?
It will be easier to remember the steps to rescue the child and you'll be able to think more clearly.

How is coughing different from choking?
Coughing is good. Coughing helps. Choking is bad. Choking requires help. Coughing is the body's attempt to get rid of anything blocking the airway. Choking occurs when coughing fails to remove the blockage and air cannot move past the blockage into or out of the lungs. The body cannot get rid of the blockage without help. Choking is a **THREAT TO LIFE** that requires immediate action.

How do abdominal thrusts clear the airway?
Correctly delivered abdominal thrusts work just like effective coughs. Both take advantage of the air trapped in the lungs below the blockage. An effective cough or abdominal thrust pushes the trapped air out of the lungs and into the airway below the blockage. If the force of the air pushing on the object is strong enough, the object will be pushed out of the airway and the airway will be cleared.

Why do I need to check the position of my hands after every 5 abdominal thrusts?
When the child is unable to breathe, the lack of oxygen can cause limpness which makes the child become heavy in your arms. The child may slip down in your arms so your hands are in the wrong place. Your abdominal thrusts may not work and you could injure the child.

What do I need to tell the employer?
Call employer after 9-1-1 arrives or if you have given abdominal thrusts. Tell employer if abdominal thrusts made the child better and the object came out or if the child got better with abdominal thrusts, but you did not see the object come out. The child should be seen by a physician.

RULES TO PREVENT CHOKING

DO be aware that children up to age 5 are most at risk for choking deaths.

DO supervise the child while the child is eating or drinking.

DO make sure the child sits while eating or drinking.

DO cut food into thin, small strips. Be sure to cut round food, like carrots, lengthwise.

DO look for objects that are a choking danger and remove from play areas.

DO be aware that food and toys safe for older children may not be safe for a younger child.

DON'T give hard candy, nuts, or popcorn to a child up to age 5.

DON'T give smooth round food like hot dogs or grapes to a child up to age 5.

DON'T give food that can ball up and get stuck in the back of the mouth like peanut butter or marshmallows to a child up to age 5.

DON'T tickle or get the child excited when the child is eating.

DON'T allow the child to play with latex balloons, coins, marbles, or small balls.

DON'T allow the child to play with or put any object smaller than the child's fist in mouth.

Choking Infant Rescue

UNDER 1 YEAR

Coughing Helps!

Stay with the infant and be ready to rescue if the infant:

- puts food or other object in mouth and begins to cough
- has sudden difficulty breathing—especially if the infant is coughing

Choking Requires Help!

Act immediately if the infant:

- is unable to breathe
- is unable to make a noise when trying to cough, cry, or talk
- has high-pitched, noisy breathing or is making gagging sound
- has bluish lips or skin is pale, blue, or grayish

1. **Allow the infant to cough. Do not pat or slap the infant on the back.**
2. **Prepare to give back blows and chest thrusts if the infant becomes unable to cough or talk, or if cough becomes very weak.**
3. **Ask anyone who can to call 9-1-1 for help.** If you are alone, do not delay rescue attempts to make the call.
4. **Get in position to give back blows and chest thrusts.** Sit on the edge of a chair and form a ramp by placing your legs together and straightening them out in front of you. Make a V with one hand. Put the V on the infant's jawbone. Using your hand and forearm to provide firm support for the infant's chin, neck and upper chest, place the infant in a face-down position on your arm which is resting on your thigh.
5. **Give up to 5 back blows.** Using the heel of your free hand, give up to 5 firm, forceful back blows between the infant's shoulder blades. Count out loud, "One! Two! Three! Four! Five!"
6. **Turn the infant to face-up position** if the object does not come out after 5 back blows. While supporting the infant's head and neck with your hands, sandwich the infant's body between your arms and roll the infant onto your other thigh so the infant is face-up. **Keep the infant's head lower than its chest at all times.**
7. **Give up to 5 chest thrusts.** Quickly remove or arrange clothes so you can see the infant's chest. Place two fingers of your free hand on the infant's breastbone just below the nipple line and give up to 5 quick, firm downward chest thrusts. Say out loud, "Cough! Cough! Cough! Cough! Cough!"
8. **Turn the infant to face-down position.**
9. **Repeat steps 5, 6, 7, and 8.**
10. **Don't give up.** Continue giving back blows and chest thrusts supporting the head and neck during turns until the object is "coughed out" and the infant can breathe, cough, or cry or until the infant stops responding or loses consciousness.
11. **If the infant loses consciousness, take infant with you and call 9-1-1** for further instructions.
12. **If the infant begins to breathe, cough, or cry, stop giving back blows and chest thrusts.**
13. **Always call employer after 9-1-1 arrives** or if you have given back blows and chest thrusts.

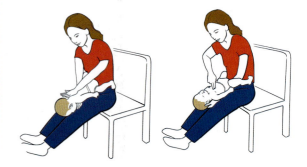

Understanding Choking Infant Rescue

How can I protect an infant from choking?
The best protection is prevention. Watch the infant! Watch for danger!

Why is it important for me to stay calm?
It will be easier to remember the steps to rescue the infant and you'll be able to think more clearly.

How is coughing different from choking?
Coughing is good. Coughing helps. Choking is bad. Choking requires help. Coughing is the body's attempt to get rid of anything blocking the airway. Choking occurs when coughing fails to remove the blockage and air cannot move past the blockage into or out of the lungs. The body cannot get rid of the blockage without help. Choking is a **THREAT TO LIFE** that requires immediate action.

How do back blows and chest thrusts clear the airway?
Back blows can cause the airway to briefly loosen its grip on the object and the object may be loose enough to move in the airway. Chest thrusts are "substitute coughs." Chest thrusts squeeze the lungs causing air trapped below the blockage to push the object out toward the mouth. Chest thrusts must be quick and forceful in order to create enough pressure to "cough" the blockage out.

Why must the infant's head be lower than the chest at all times?
With back blows, the infant's head must be lower than the chest so that once the object is loosened, it falls toward the mouth and doesn't move deeper into the airway. With chest thrusts, keeping the head down makes it possible for gravity to help the "substitute cough" move the object toward the mouth. During turns, the head must be lower than the chest to prevent a loosened object from falling deeper into the airway.

Why shouldn't I use abdominal thrusts on an infant?
The liver, stomach, and spleen lie lower in the infant's abdomen than they do in a child or adult. The force used with abdominal thrusts may injure these fragile organs. The infant's lungs are also fragile, but they are protected from the force of chest thrusts by the rib cage.

What do I need to tell the employer?
Call employer after 9-1-1 arrives or if you have given back blows and chest thrusts. Tell employer if back blows and chest thrusts made the infant better and the object came out or if the infant got better with back blows and chest thrusts, but you did not see the object come out. The infant should be seen by a physician.

RULES TO PREVENT CHOKING

DO be aware that children up to age 5 are most at risk for choking deaths.

DO stay with the infant who is eating or drinking to watch for problems.

DO make sure the infant is sitting in a high chair or infant seat while eating or drinking.

DO give small amounts and small pieces of soft food like ripe bananas or applesauce.

DO wait until the infant has swallowed one bite before offering another.

DO examine all toys for loose parts.

DO place all small objects out of infant's reach.

DON'T give the infant hard food like candy, nuts, popcorn, raw carrots, or apples.

DON'T give the infant smooth round food like hot dogs or grapes.

DON'T give the infant food that can ball up and get stuck in the back of the mouth like peanut butter or marshmallows.

DON'T hurry the infant, tickle, or play games while the infant is eating.

DON'T allow the infant to play with latex balloons, coins, marbles, or small balls.

DON'T allow the infant to play with or put any object smaller than the infant's fist in mouth.

Child CPR

1 YEAR OR OLDER

1. **Tap the child's shoulder and call out the child's name.** Check to see if the child responds—moves, speaks, blinks, or reacts to you.
2. **If child doesn't respond, ask anyone who can to call 9-1-1 for help.** If you are alone, do not delay rescue attempts to make the call.
3. If the child is lying face-down, roll the child over to his back while carefully supporting the head and neck. Make sure the child is lying on a firm, flat surface.
4. **Check breathing.** Look from head to belly to see if child is not breathing or only gasping. If not breathing or only gasping, give CPR.
5. **Do 30 chest compressions.** Quickly remove or arrange clothes so that you can see the child's chest. Be sure the child's clothing doesn't cover his face. Place heel of one hand on the center of the child's chest between the nipples. Place the heel of your other hand on top of the first hand. Push straight down on the child's breastbone keeping your arms straight. Compress about 2 inches. Count out loud while you push hard and fast. You should push at a rate of 100–120 pushes per minute. After each push, release pressure on the chest so the chest can return to its normal position.
6. **If you know or suspect the child may have choked, open the child's mouth widely and look for an object, such as food or toy.** If you see an object, carefully remove it with your fingers.
7. **Open the airway by gently tilting the head back and lifting the chin up.** Put one hand on the forehead and two fingers of your other hand on the child's jawbone.
8. **Give 2 rescue breaths.** While holding airway open, pinch the child's nose closed. Cover the child's mouth with your mouth and create an airtight seal. Blow gently for about one second for each breath. Watch for the chest to rise as you give each breath. If the child's chest did not rise after the first breath, reposition the head using the head-tilt and chin-lift and attempt to give another breath. Proceed to chest compressions after 2 breaths even If breaths failed to cause the chest to rise.
9. **Do 30 chest compressions. Continue CPR for 2 minutes or a total of 5 sets of 30 chest compressions and 2 rescue breaths.** If you know or suspect the child may have choked, check the mouth each time you open the airway to give breaths.
10. **Call 9-1-1 and then continue doing CPR until 9-1-1 arrives and takes over or until the child starts to breathe and move.** If the child begins to breathe but is still not responding, roll the child onto his side with head tilted slightly back. Stay with the child and wait for 9-1-1 to arrive. If the child stops breathing, roll the child to his back and resume CPR.
11. **Call employer after 9-1-1 arrives.**

Understanding Child CPR

How can I protect a child from a THREAT TO LIFE?
Prevention is the best protection. Watch the child! Watch for danger!

What do the letters in CPR stand for?
C stands for cardio which refers to the heart. P stands for pulmonary which refers to the lungs. R stands for resuscitation which refers to rescue. CPR is used to rescue a heart and lungs that are not working.

What kinds of problems might a child have that would require me to do CPR?
Most children who need CPR are unable to breathe as a result of choking, drowning, suffocation, or severe head injury.

How do chest compressions help?
Chest compressions act like a "substitute heart." Pressing on the heart squeezes blood out of the heart and into the arteries to take it around the body. Push hard and fast so the "substitute heart" can do its job. Release the pressure after each push so blood can refill the heart. Do not stop giving chest compressions except for a few seconds to give breaths.

How does the head tilt/chin-lift open the airway?
Tilting the child's head back slightly straightens the airway making it easier for air to move in and out of the lungs. Tilting the head back too far kinks the airway and closes it off. A slightly bigger child needs a slightly bigger tilt. Lifting the jaw upward with the chin-lift prevents the tongue from blocking the airway by moving it away from the back of the throat. Be sure you lift the chin by lifting on the jawbone. Pressure on the soft part of the neck or under the chin may close off the child's airway.

How do rescue breaths help?
Rescue breaths are extremely important for children who need CPR. After you have the blood circulating by doing chest compressions, you need to give the child more oxygen to stay alive. Only blow hard enough to make the child's chest rise slightly. A slightly bigger child needs a slightly bigger breath. Your mouth must completely cover the child's mouth while you pinch the child's nose closed to prevent your breath from escaping.

WHAT IS AN AED?

An AED is an Automated External Defibrillator. When victims collapse and need CPR, AEDs are often used to analyze and correct an abnormal heart rhythm.

AEDs can now be found in many public places such as schools, sports facilities, and restaurants. If you are on the phone with 9-1-1, they may ask if you have access to an AED.

Infant CPR

UNDER 1 YEAR

1. **Tap or gently jiggle infant's foot and call out infant's name.** Check to see if the infant responds—moves, makes sounds, blinks, or reacts to you.
2. **If the infant doesn't respond, ask anyone who can to call 9-1-1 for help.** If you are alone, do not delay rescue attempts to make the call.
3. If infant is lying face-down, make a V with one hand. Put the V on the back of the infant's head to support the head and neck while you carefully roll infant over to her back. Move infant to a firm, flat surface like a table.
4. **Check breathing.** Look from head to belly to see if infant is not breathing or only gasping. If not breathing or only gasping, give CPR.
5. **Do 30 chest compressions.** Quickly remove or arrange clothes so that you can see the infant's chest. Be sure infant's clothing doesn't cover her face. Place two fingers of one hand just below the nipple line. Make sure your fingers are well above the lower end of the breastbone. Push straight down on infant's breastbone. Compress about 1½ inches. Count out loud while you push hard and fast. You should push at a rate of 100-120 pushes per minute. After each push, release pressure on the chest so the chest can return to its normal position.
6. **If you know or suspect the infant may have choked, open the infant's mouth widely and look for an object, such as food or toy.** If you see an object, carefully remove it with your fingers.
7. **Open the airway** by gently tilting the head back and lifting the chin up. Put one hand on the forehead and two fingers of your other hand on the infant's jawbone.
8. **Give 2 rescue breaths.** While holding airway open, cover the infant's mouth and nose with your mouth and create an airtight seal by pressing your lips firmly against the infant's face. Blow gently about one second for each breath. Watch for the chest to rise as you give each breath. If the infant's chest did not rise after the first breath, reposition the head using the head-tilt and chin-lift and attempt to give another breath. Proceed to chest compressions after 2 breaths even if breaths failed to cause the chest to rise.
9. **Do 30 chest compressions. Continue CPR for 2 minutes or a total of 5 sets of 30 chest compressions and 2 rescue breaths.** If you know or suspect the infant may have choked, check the mouth each time you open the airway to give breaths.
10. **Call 9-1-1 and then continue doing CPR until 9-1-1 arrives and takes over or until the infant starts to breathe and move.** If the infant begins to breathe but is still not responding, roll the infant onto her side with head tilted slightly back. Stay with the infant and wait for 9-1-1 to arrive. If the infant stops breathing, roll the infant to her back and resume CPR.
11. **Call employer after 9-1-1 arrives.**

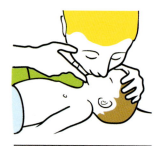

Understanding Infant CPR

How can I protect an infant from a THREAT TO LIFE?
Prevention is the best protection. Watch the infant! Watch for danger!

What do the letters in CPR stand for?
C stands for cardio which refers to the heart. P stands for pulmonary which refers to the lungs. R stands for resuscitation which refers to rescue. CPR is used to rescue a heart and lungs that are not working.

What kinds of problems might an infant have that would require me to do CPR?
Most infants who need CPR are unable to breathe as a result of choking, sudden infant death syndrome (unexplained death of a sleeping infant in the first year of life—cause unknown), drowning, or suffocation.

How do chest compressions help?
Chest compressions act like a "substitute heart." Pressing on the heart squeezes blood out of the heart and into the arteries to take it around the body. Push hard and fast so the "substitute heart" can do its job. Release the pressure after each push so blood can refill the heart. Do not stop giving chest compressions except for a few seconds to give breaths.

How does the head tilt/chin-lift open the airway?
Tilting the infant's head back slightly straightens the airway making it easier for air to move in and out of the lungs. Tilting the head back too far kinks the airway and closes it off. A teeny-tiny infant needs a teeny-tiny tilt. Lifting the jaw upward with the chin-lift prevents the tongue from blocking the airway by moving it away from the back of the throat. Be sure you lift the chin by lifting on the jawbone. Pressure on the soft part of the neck or under the chin may close off the infant's airway.

How do rescue breaths help?
Rescue breaths are extremely important for infants who need CPR. After you have the blood circulating by doing chest compressions, you need to give the infant more oxygen to stay alive. Only blow hard enough to make the infant's chest rise slightly. A teeny-tiny infant needs a teeny-tiny breath. Your mouth must completely cover the infant's nose and mouth to prevent your breath from escaping. If you can't do that, put your mouth over the infant's nose and give breaths through the infant's nose while you hold the infant's mouth closed.

WHY IS C-A-B HELPFUL TO REMEMBER?

C-A-B stands for Compressions, Airway, and Breathing. If you need to provide CPR on an infant or child, C-A-B can help you remember in which order to provide rescue skills.

After checking for breathing you should provide 30 Compressions, open the Airway, and then provide 2 rescue Breaths.

Review

What are some common safety hazards for children of all ages?

Why does a THREAT TO LIFE require a call to 9-1-1?

What is the difference between coughing and choking?

When do you use back blows and chest thrusts to rescue someone who is choking?

When do you use abdominal thrusts?

LIFE & BUSINESS SKILLS

Whether you are babysitting, mowing lawns, or doing odd jobs for family or friends, success on the job depends on three things: being prepared, being responsible, and being considerate. These things are the keys to success.

IT'S OKAY TO DISCUSS MONEY

If you are babysitting or doing other jobs for family, neighbors, or others you know, you will need to set your fee. Decide how much you are going to charge for a job before you talk to an employer. Make your fee fair – not too high and not too low. When you discuss a job opportunity with an employer, let them know how much you charge.

Be Prepared

When you are presented with a job opportunity, it's important that you are prepared to take on that job. You don't need to say yes to every request. To decide which jobs to accept and which to refuse, you need to screen every job ASAP.

A – Am I Available?
Is that date saved for family, friends, school, or another job? Do I have a lot to do that week?

S – Will I be Safe?
Do I have a safe way to get back and forth? Does the employer make me uncomfortable? Is the home in a safe neighborhood? Will there be a phone available for me? Is the home safe for my health? For example, am I allergic to their pets?

A – Am I Able?
If babysitting, are there more than 2 children? Is the child younger than 6 months old? Does the child have a medical problem? Is the job too long? Are there extra responsibilities?

P – Do I have Permission?
Does my parent have all the information needed to make a good decision about me accepting this job? Do I know the details of the job (Who/What/Where/When/How) so that I can share them with my parent?

Screening a Job

1. How do you spell your name? What is your phone number and address?

2. When do you need someone? What time will you be leaving/returning?

3. How many children and what are their ages? Are there any special issues or extra responsibilities I should know about? Are you willing to provide transportation?

4. I charge $_____ an hour. Will that be okay?

5. How did you hear about me? Did someone refer you to me?

6. I will need to check to be sure that I can accept this job. Can I call or text you back tonight?

THE HIGH FIVE INFO: WHO, WHAT, WHERE, WHEN, HOW

WHO is my employer? Note the first and last name, including the spelling, as well as a phone number.

WHAT type of job is it? If babysitting, note the names and ages of the kids.

WHERE is the job? Note the full address.

WHEN is the job? Note the date and time.

HOW will I get to and from the job? Note if you will need transportation and who will be providing that.

Next Steps

1. Always check with the person who referred you. Your name might be given out because you are a good babysitter, not because the person who referred you thinks you should actually take the job.
2. Next, discuss the job offer with your parent.
3. If you are Available, will be Safe, are Able, and have your parent's Permission, then call the employer back to make final arrangements.
4. Make arrangements for a back-up adult who will be available to provide immediate help, if needed.
5. Make sure you will have access to a phone (either a cell phone or landline).
6. Remember to make time for a house tour and information gathering with a new employer.
7. Share the High Five info (Who/What/Where/When/How) with your parent.

Refusing a Job

If you feel you should not accept a job, here are some good things to say:

> I'm sorry I can't accept the job because I don't feel comfortable babysitting for such a long time.

If the job is too long

> I'm sorry I can't accept the job because I don't feel comfortable babysitting for a child so young.

If the child is too young

> I'm sorry I can't accept the job because I don't think I could handle cooking and watching the children.

If there are extra responsibilities

> I'm sorry I can't accept the job because I don't feel comfortable babysitting for so many children.

If there are too many children

> I'm sorry I can't accept the job because I don't have a safe way to get back and forth to your house and I'm not allowed to ride my bike after dark.

If it is an unsafe situation

> I'm sorry but I can't accept the job because I have trouble handling bedtime with your children. Maybe you need a babysitter who is older.

If you have difficulty getting the children to listen or follow the rules

If you're not comfortable saying any of the above or if the reference doesn't check out, you can always say:

> I am sorry but I'm not available.

If you are going to refuse the job offer, **CALL PROMPTLY** to let the employer know. Leave a message if you cannot reach them. Do not text unless they have asked you to let them know via text.

Be Responsible

Dress appropriately for the job.
Appropriate clothes for a babysitting job are clothes that are clean and will let you comfortably move around and play with a young child. Avoid anything that might be dangerous around a young child such as dangling earrings, breakable jewelry, or studs and chains. Avoid clothing that is revealing. It's smart to wear washable clothing. Have long hair pulled back and be sure you don't have long fingernails.

Don't carry things in your purse, backpack, or pockets that could harm a young child. Any product or substance that can harm someone if used in the wrong way, by the wrong person, or in the wrong amount is a poison. Some examples are medicines you swallow like pills or medicines you put on your skin like acne preparations, cosmetics like perfume or nail polish, and batteries, especially small batteries.

Be ready to go.
Be ready 5 to 10 minutes early if you are going to be picked up. If you are getting to the job on your own, be sure to arrive on time. Don't be late. Remember to arrange additional time for orientation.

VISIT SAFESITTER.ORG TO DOWNLOAD THE SAFE SITTER® HELP SHEET TO YOUR PHONE OR TABLET.

Take notes!
It takes about 10 minutes with a repeat employer and 30 minutes with a new employer for you to discuss what you need to know to take care of the children and to learn the rules of the house. Take notes on the following:

- **Important Information:**
  Write down the employer's name, phone number, and address, as well as the name and phone number of a back-up adult.
- **Children's Routines:**
  Be sure to write down the name and age of each child. Don't forget to ask how to handle problem behavior and how to comfort the child if necessary.
- **House Tour/Responsibilities:**
  Ask the employer to take you on a tour of the house. Be sure you know the family's fire escape plan and location of outside meeting place. Ask the employer if any food in the refrigerator or pantry is off-limits, for you or for the child. Ask about house rules for the children, including rules regarding the use of the television and electronic games and devices. Be sure to ask about pet routines.

Make sure you have access to a phone.
A phone is a tool for communication—not a distraction. The employer must be able to reach you at all times, but let other calls and messages go unanswered. After the child is asleep you can use your cell phone and other electronic devices for personal use.

After the Job
Employers are interested in hearing how things went while they were gone. If the child is not yet talking, you are the only one who can provide that information. Be sure to tell the employer how snacks/meals and bedtime/naps went. The employer will especially appreciate hearing about something funny, cute, or smart that the child did. You'll find yourself smiling when you tell it.

Be Considerate

When you are babysitting, you are a guest in the employer's home.

- **DON'T** allow your friends to come over. If they drop by, tell them they can't come in and you can't talk.
- **DON'T** go through drawers or private areas of the home.
- **DON'T** share that you are babysitting, tag your location, or post photos of the children on social media.
- **DO** limit TV to employer-approved shows that you watch with the child.
- **DO** keep the house in good shape, like you found it. Put away toys, and wash the dishes you used.
- **DO** stay awake until at least 10:30 p.m. Then, if you need to nap, don't get too comfortable.

When You Have to Cancel

If you must cancel, give as much notice as possible.

You should only cancel if you have an appropriate reason such as an illness or family emergency, and you should only express interest in future jobs if you'd like to babysit for them.

> "I'm very sorry, but I won't be able to babysit for you because I am sick today. I can give you the name of my friend who is also a Safe Sitter® graduate. I hope you'll call me next time you need a babysitter."

Canceling a Job

Remember Your Manners

Be polite, respectful, and kind when meeting employers and their families.

Greeting Employer

- When you are meeting an employer for the first time, introduce yourself.
- Look the employer right in the eye. Smile.
- Speak clearly and loudly enough that you can be heard and understood without being asked to repeat yourself.
- Shake hands firmly with the employer.

Greeting Children

- Greet each person in the room. Each child, no matter what age, should be addressed by name.
- Be sure to smile at the child. Show your interest in a young child by saying something like "He's so cute" or "She really loves that bear, doesn't she?"
- Get down to the child's eye level when you are talking to the child.
- Make conversation with an older child. You can ask what the child is doing or ask the child's age or name.
- Don't be embarrassed to show that you like children.

Review

What are the three keys to success on the job?

What does ASAP stand for?

What is the High Five info?

Why should you bring a cell phone to a babysitting or other job?